A Visit to
ITALY

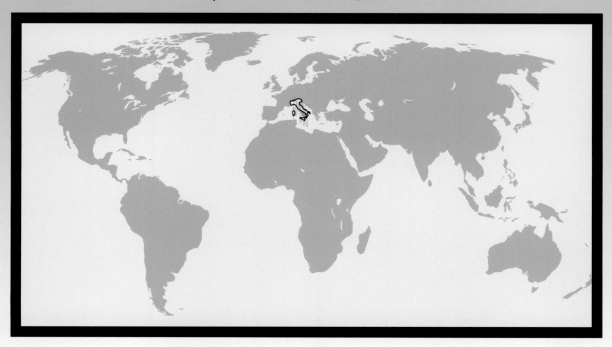

Rachael Bell

Heinemann Library
Des Plaines, Illinois

© 1999 Reed Educational & Professional Publishing
Published by Heinemann Library,
an imprint of Reed Educational & Professional Publishing,
1350 East Touhy Avenue, Suite 240 West
Des Plaines, IL 60018

Customer Service 1-888-454-2279

Designed by AMR
Illustrations by Art Construction
Printed in Hong Kong/China

03 02 01 00 99
10 9 8 7 6 5 4 3 2 1

Library of Congress Cataloging-in-Publication Data

Bell, Rachael, 1972-
    A visit to Italy / Rachael Bell
        p. cm. – (A visit to)
    Includes bibliographical references and index.
    Summary: Introduces the land, landmarks, homes, food, clothes, work, transportation, language, schools, recreation, and culture of Italy.
    ISBN 1-57572-853-2 (lib. bdg.)
    1. Italy—Juvenile literature. [1. Italy.] I. Title.
II. Title: Italy. III. Series.
DG417.B45 1999
945—dc21   99-18085
                                                      CIP

Acknowledgments
The Publishers would like to thank the following for permission to reproduce photographs:
Axel Poignant Archive/Ali Reale, p. 29; Colorific/David Levenson/Black Star, p. 22; Colorsport, p. 24; Hutchison Library/J. Davey, p. 23; Isabella Tree, p. 25; J. Allan Cash, pp. 9, 17, 21; Katz Pictures/A. Tosatto, p. 14; Performing Arts Library, Gianfranco Fainello, p. 28; Robert Francis, p. 18; Robert Harding Picture Library/Mike Newton, pp. 12, 20; Spectrum Color Library, p. 13; Stock Market, p. 10; Telegraph Color Library, pp. 8; C. Chinca, p. 5; J. Sims, pp. 6, 16; Tony Stone/Joe Cornish, p. 11; Trevor Clifford, pp. 12, 16; Trip/R. Cracknell, p. 7; P. Nicholas, p. 15; W. Jacobs, pp. 20, 26; H. Rogers, p. 27.

Cover photo: Telegraph Colour Library /A. Tilley

Any words appearing in bold, **like this**, are explained in the Glossary.

Contents

Italy

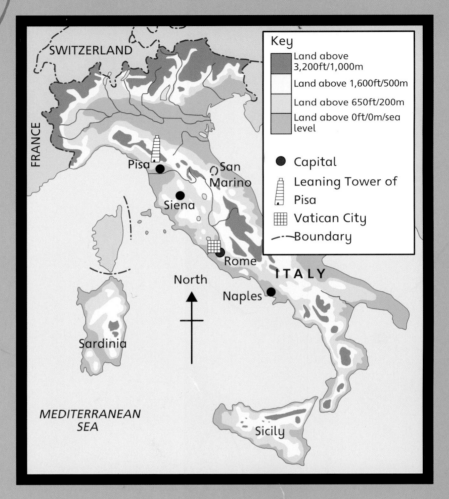

Italy is in southern Europe. The shape of the country is like a boot in the Mediterranean Sea. The islands of Sicily and Sardinia are also part of Italy.

Two places inside Italy, the Vatican City and San Marino, are not part of Italy. Italians eat, sleep, play, and go to school like you. Italian life is also **unique**.

Land

Most of the land in Italy is mountains or hills. These areas have only thin **soil**. Many plants cannot grow in thin soil. This makes farming difficult.

The highest mountains are in northern Italy. The mountains have snow on them all year round. In the south it is much hotter. There is very little rain.

Landmarks

One of Italy's most famous buildings is the Leaning Tower of Pisa. It is over 800 years old. There are 294 steps to the top.

Rome is the capital of Italy. The Vatican City is like a small town inside the city of Rome. It is the home of the **Pope**. There is beautiful art here.

Homes

Most people in Italy live in towns or cities. This is the city of Naples. It grew up around a busy **port**. People left the **rural** areas to come here for work.

In the country, most houses have some
land around them. Here people can grow
food for themselves or to sell.

Food

Many families enjoy eating together.
They might eat cold meats with salad,
pasta, bread, and cheese for lunch.

Many delicious foods come from Italy. Pizza first came from Naples. Now most towns have a **pizzeria**.

Clothes

Young people wear clothes like yours.

Some of the older people wear black.
This shows that they are in **mourning**.

Work

Some people work in farming. They grow grapes, wheat, fruit, and vegetables. Oranges are grown on this farm in Sicily.

In central and southern Italy, many people work in shops and offices. They close around noon for **siesta**, because the weather is hot. **Products**, such as cars or engines, are made in the north.

Transportation

Italy has good roads and highways. It also has very good train service. There are **ports** and airports too. Many young people ride **scooters**.

Gondolas are used for transportation in Venice. Venice has **canals** instead of streets. Gondolas help people get around.

Italy's official language is Italian.
Italian comes from the ancient
language of Latin.

The other main language in Italy is Sardinian. This is spoken by people on the island of Sardinia. People in some **regions** in Italy speak their own **dialect**.

School

Elementary school is for children from six to eleven years old. School starts at 8:30 A.M. and finishes at 1:00 P.M. Students go to school six days a week.

Middle school is for eleven to fourteen year olds. Their school day is longer. They usually have sports after school. Some students go to high school.

Free Tim

Most Italians love soccer. People of all ages talk about it and play it. There are soccer games on Sunday afternoons.

In the early evenings people meet and walk around the main **square** or street in their town. This walk is called the *passeggiata* (pass-eh-jee-ah-tah).

Celebrations

Every town in Italy has at least one festival. People take the day off work or school to watch a **procession** through the town.

On July 2 and August 16, there is a bareback horse race in Siena. Before the race, people parade around the main **square** in costumes.

The Arts

Many Italians enjoy **opera**. Italy has many opera singers. Some of the operas take place in **stadiums** that were built long ago by the **ancient Romans**.

The Punch and Judy puppet show started in Italy hundreds of years ago. Today puppet shows are still very popular in Sicily.

Fact File

Name   The full name for Italy is the Italian Republic.
Capital   The **capital** of Italy is Rome.
Languages   Italy has two official languages: Italian and
                Sardinian.
Population About 58 million people live in Italy.
Money   Italian money is called lira.
Religions   Almost all Italians are Roman Catholic.
Products   Italy produces wheat, vegetables, olives,
                machines, and clothing.

Words You Can Learn

uno (oono)	one
due (do-eh)	two
tre (tray)	three
si (see)	yes
non (noh)	no
buon giorno (bwon jorno)	hello
arrivederci (a-re-va-der-che)	goodbye
per favore (per-faVOR-eh)	please
grazie (grat-zi)	thank you

Glossary

ancient Romans	People who ruled most of Europe over 2,000 years ago. The center of their goverment was in Rome.
canal	River dug by people
capital	City where the government is based
dialect	Special way people in one area say and use the words of their language
gondola	Long, narrow boat used on the canals in Venice
mourning	The wearing of black clothing to show sadness for someone's death
opera	Play with music and singing
pasta	Kind of dough made from flour, and then shaped, dried, and cooked in boiling water. Spaghetti is a kind of pasta.
Pope	Head of the Roman Catholic Church
port	Place where ships pick up and drop off the goods they are carrying
pizzeria	Place where you can buy pizza
procession	Group of people walking along behind each other and often wearing costumes
product	Thing that is grown, taken from the earth, made by hand, or made in a factory
region	Area or part of a country
rural	The country, not the city
scooter	Small-wheeled motorbike
siesta	Time for people to rest during the middle of the day
soil	Ground that plants grow in
square	Open space in a city with streets on all four sides
stadium	Large field surrounded by seats
unique	Different in a special way

Index

More Books to Read

Arnold, Helen. *Italy*. Chatham, NJ: Raintree Steck-Vaughn, 1996.

Clark, Colin. *Journey Through Italy*. Mahwah, NJ: Troll Communications, 1997. An older reader can help you with this book.

Lerner Publications, Department of Geography Staff. *Italy – In Pictures*. Lerner Publishing Group, 1997.